ISBN 0 947338 82 9

Victorian
Cottage Garden

From Come Hither

Art weary? Here's the place
For weariness to rest,
These flowers are herbs of
grace
To cure the aching breast;
Soft beds these mossy banks
where dewdrops only weep,
where Nature turns God
thanks
And sings herself to sleep.
Art troubled with strife?
Come hither,
Here's peace and summer
weather.

John Clare (1793-1864)

The Herb Garden.

Flowers always make people
better, happier, and more
helpful;
they are sunshine, food and
medicine to the soul.

Luther Burbank

What wondrous life is
this I lead!
Ripe apples drop about
my head;
The luscious clusters
of the vine
Upon my mouth do
crust their wine;
The nectarine,
and curious peach,
In to my hands themselves
do reach;
Stumbling on melons,
as I pass,
Ensnared with flowers,
I fall on grass.

Andrew Marvell (1621-1678)

PICTURESQUE DORSET.
Wool Bridge and Manor House.

I have a garden of my own
But so with roses overgrown
And lillies, that you would it
guess
To be a little wilderness.

Andrew Marvell (1621–1678)

THATCHED COTTAGES.
BLACKPOOL SANDS, S.DEVON

A violet by a mossy stone
Half hidden from the eye,
Fair as a star,
when only one
Is shining in the sky.

William Wordsworth (1770-1850)

THE REST, SELWORTHY

The kiss of the sun for
pardon,
The song of the birds for
mirth,
One is nearer God's heart
in the garden
Than anywhere else on earth.

Dorothy Frances Gurney
(1858-1932)

Last night, there came
a frost, which has done
great damage to my garden...

It is sad that nature will
play such tricks
with us poor mortals,
inviting us with sunny
smiles to confide in her,
and then,
when we are entirely within
her power,
striking us to the heart.

Nathaniel Hawthorne
(1804-1864)

From the Secret Garden

Mistress Mary worked in
her garden until it was time
to go to her midday dinner.
In fact, she was rather late in
remembering, and when she
put on her coat and hat, and
picked up her skipping-rope,
she could not believe that she
had been working two or
three hours. She had been
actually happy all the time;
and dozens and dozens of
the tiny, pale-green points
were to be seen in cleared

places, looking twice as cheerful as they had looked before when the grass and weeds had be smothering them. "I shall come back this afternoon," she said, looking all round at her new kingdom, and speaking to the trees and the rosebushes as if they heard her. Then she ran lightly across the grass, pushed open the slow old door, and slipped through it under the ivy.

Frances Hodgson Burnett

By all those token flowers
that tell
what words can never speak
so well.

Lord Byron (1788-1824)

The Cottage Homes of England
WELFORD-ON-AVON.

A·R·QUINTON

To cultivate a Garden is to walk with God.

Christian Bovee

The garden admires you.
For your sake it smears itself
with green pigment,
the ecstatic reds of the roses,
so that you will come to it
with your lovers.

Louise Geluk

A Surrey Cottage.

From The Affectionate
Shepherd

Nay more than this, I have a
garden plot,
Wherein there wants nor
herbs, nor roots, nor flowers
(Flowers to smell, roots to eat,
herbs for the pot),
And dainty shelters when the
welkin lours;
Sweet smelling beds of lillies
and of roses
Which rosemary banks and
lavendar encloses.

Richard Barnfield (1574–1627)

ARTS GUILD COTTAGE
BROCKENHURST

I knew by the smoke that so
gracefully curled
Above the green elms, that a
cottage was near,
And I said, 'If there's peace to
be found in the world,
A heart that was humble
might hope for it here.'

Thomas Moore (1779-1852)

If you truly love Nature, you will find beauty everywhere.

Vincent van Gogh

ANNE HATHAWAY'S COTTAGE.

The Sundial

'Tis an old dial, dark with
many a stain;
In summer crowned with
drifting orchard bloom,
Tricked in the autumn with
the yellow rain,
And white in winter like a
marble tomb.

Henry Austin Dobson

Nature never did betray
The heart that loved her.

william wordsworth

PICTURESQUE DORSET
Hangman's Cottage, Dorchester

It is the month of June
The month of leaves and
roses,
when pleasant sights salute
the eyes
And pleasant scents the
noses.

Nathanial Parker Willis
(1806-1894)

PICTURESQUE DORSET.
The Mill & Church, Affpuddle, Dorchester.

Eutopia

There is a garden where lilies
And roses are side by side;
And all day between them in
silence
The silken butterflies glide.

I may not enter the garden,
Though I know the road
thereto;
And morn by morn to the
gateway
I see the children go.

They bring back light on
their faces;
But they cannot bring back to
me
What the lilies say to the
roses
Or the songs of the butterflies
be.

Francis Turner Palgrave
(1824–1897)

And time remembered
is grief forgotten
And frosts are slain
and flowers begotten
And in green underwood
and cover
Blossom by blossom
the Spring begins.

A C Swinburne (1837-1909)

*One touch of nature makes
the whole world kin.*

William Shakespeare

The Secret Garden

The sun was shining inside
the four walls and the high
arch of blue sky over this
particular piece of
Misselthwaite seemed even
more brilliant and soft than
it was over the moor. The
robin flew down from his
tree-top and hopped about or
flew after her from one bush
to another. He chirped a good
deal and had a very busy air,
as if he were showing her
things. Everything was
strange and silent and she
seemed to be hundreds of

miles away from anyone, but somehow she did not feel lonely at all. All that troubled her was her wish that she knew whether all the roses were dead, or if perhaps some of them had lived and might put out leaves and buds as the weather got warmer. She did not want it to be a quite dead garden. If it were a quite alive garden, how wonderful it would be, and what thousands of roses would grow on every side!

From My Mother's Garden

Forget-me-knots there
linger,
To full perfection brought,
And there bloom purple
pansies
In many a tender thought.
There love's own roses
blossom,
As from enchanted ground,
And lavish perfume exquisite
The whole glad year around.

And in that quiet garden –
The garden of her heart –
Songbirds are always
singing
Their songs of cheer apart.

Alice E Allen

The greatest gift of the
garden
is the restoration of the five
senses.

Hanna Rion

*Everywhere the lanes were
fragrant with Wild Roses,
and honeysuckle and the
breeze came to us over the
hedges laden with the
perfume of the clover-fields
and grass-meadows.*

Edith Holden (1871-1920)

*Flowers are the sweetest
things
God ever made and forgot to
put a soul into.*

Henry Ward Beecher
(1813–1887)

BERKSHIRE LANE